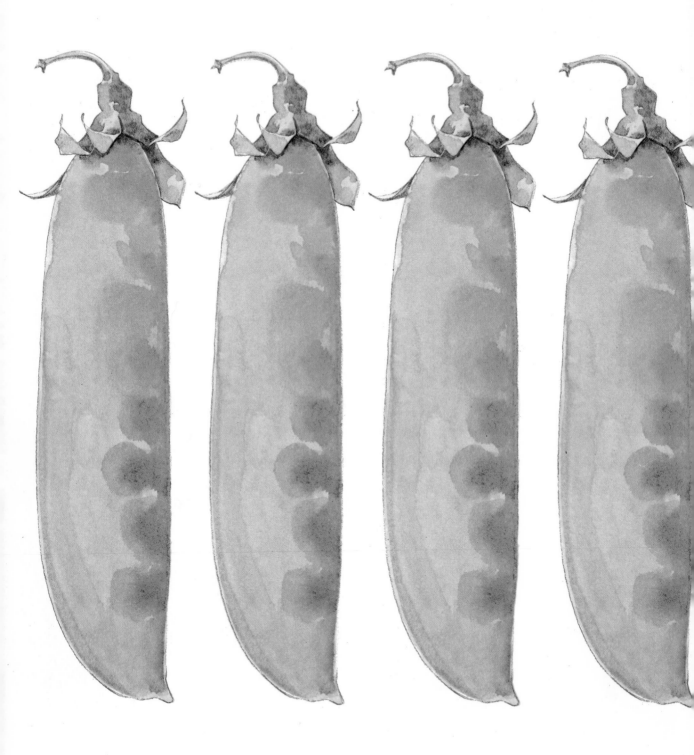

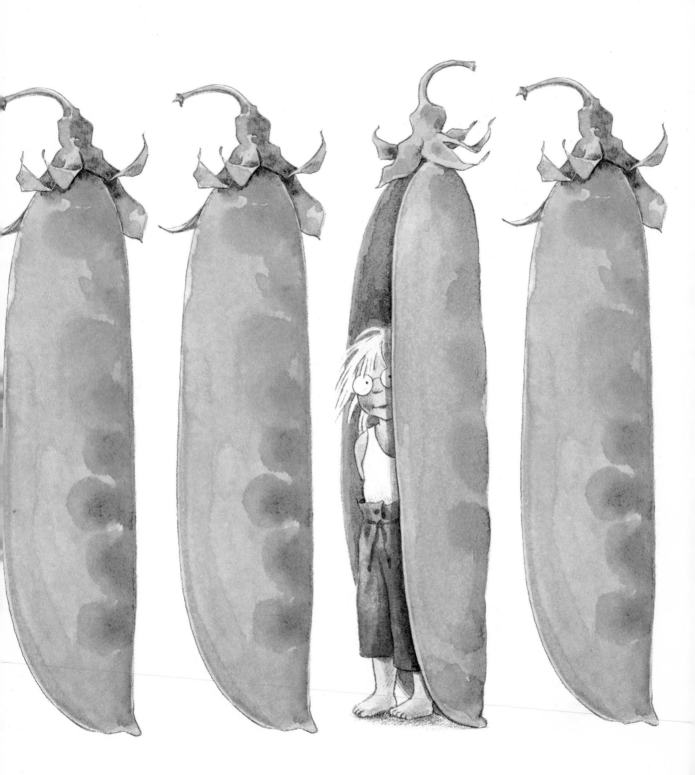

ANNA'S GARDEN SONGS

Pictures by Lena Anderson
Poems by Mary Q. Steele

Greenwillow Books New York

The pictures are for Nicolina
—L. A.

Once again the words in this book are for
Melissa Christine, with lots of love
—M. Q. S.

Text copyright © 1989 by Mary Q. Steele.
Illustrations copyright © 1987 by Lena Anderson.
First published in Sweden in 1987
by Rabén & Sjögren as *Majas Lilla Gröna*,
with text and illustrations by Lena Anderson.
All rights reserved. No part of this book
may be reproduced or utilized in any form
or by any means, electronic or mechanical,
including photocopying, recording or by
any information storage and retrieval
system, without permission in writing
from the Publisher, Greenwillow Books,
a division of William Morrow & Company, Inc.,
105 Madison Avenue, New York, N.Y. 10016.
Printed in Italy First Edition 10 9 8 7 6 5 4 3 2 1

Library of Congress Cataloging-in-Publication Data
Steele, Mary Q.
Anna's garden songs / pictures by Lena Anderson;
poems by Mary Q. Steele.
p.   cm.
"First published in 1987 in Sweden by Rabén & Sjögren
as Majas lilla gröna, with text and illustrations by
Lena Anderson"—T.p. verso.
Summary: A collection of fourteen poems about the beet,
potato, radish, onion, and other plants found in the garden.
ISBN 0-688-08217-3.   ISBN 0-688-08218-1 (lib. bdg.)
1. Gardens—Juvenile poetry.
2. Children's poetry, American.
[1. Vegetables—Poetry. 2. Plants—Poetry.
3. Gardens—Poetry. 4. American poetry.]
I. Anderson, Lena, ill.   II. Anderson, Lena.
Majas lilla gröna   III. Title.
PS3569.T33843A817 1989
811'.54—dc19   88-5660   CIP   AC

Contents

I do not think I'll eat
This beet.
Too much of it is red,
Too much of it is head.
I do not think I'll eat
This beet.

BEET

Grandfather said:
"Here's some news for you lasses.
Potatoes have eyes
But they don't wear glasses.
They don't go to sleep,
They shed no tears,
They have no chins,
They have no ears.
Their skins are brown,
They have no curls.
Now remember this, girls."
    . . . Silly Grandfather.

POTATO

This rhubarb leaf above my head
Is big enough to cast a shade.
The leaf is green, the stem is red,
And yesterday my mother made
A rhubarb tart for us to eat.
The crust was good, the filling sweet.
But still I think that after all
It makes a better parasol.

RHUBARB

When radishes are growing
Just their green leaves are showing.
It really is a great surprise
(My rabbit can't believe his eyes)
To find their roots as rosy red
As roses in a flower bed.

RADISH

Grandfather's lettuces are good—
So fresh and crisp and green.
We eat them every day at meals
And sometimes in between.

Grandfather's lettuces are good.
I like them—but good grief!
Another bite and I may turn
Into a lettuce leaf!

LETTUCE

The fennel is the carrot's friend.
They walk together hand-in-hand.
They look about, enjoy the sun.
They think the whole wide world is fun.
It's prettier by far, they've found,
Above the grass than underground.
It happened just an hour ago
(That's when I dug them up, you know),
And now I think I'd rather not
Drop them in the supper pot!

CARROT AND FENNEL

Peas you sow in early May
Will clamber up a curly way
And bloom for you some pearly day
When rain comes down a swirly way.

And when the sun comes out to shine
Pods will grow about the vine
And fatten up—all stout and fine.

Then what delicious peas there'll be
For you to eat—and me! and me!

MAY 12   MAY 18   MAY 24

JUNE 6

Pea

JULY 20

17

Tomatoes in our garden grow
On bamboo stakes all in a row.
It's strange, but when they're served for lunch
All ripe and red, I have a hunch—
And Peter says he thinks so, too—
They won't taste one bit like bamboo.

TOMATO

Peter and I
Are in this tree
Picking cherries,
One, two, three...
Twenty, thirty, forty more,
Cherries on this tree
Galore!
Seventy, eighty, ninety-one,
Oh, this picking will
Never be done!
We'll pick until the moon comes up
And then I think
We'll have
To stop.

CHERRY

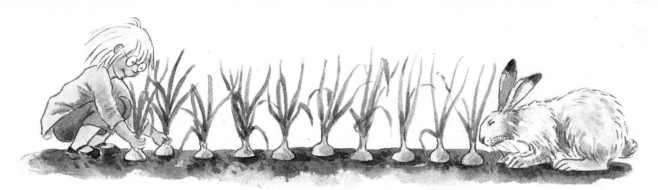

We grew so many onions
That we couldn't eat them all.
I'll braid the leaves together
And hang them on the wall.

They make a pretty ornament,
With skins of golden brown,
A cheerful thing in winter
When snow is coming down.

Mother will cut them, two by two.
We'll eat them, one by one.
And every bite will taste as sweet
As summer's shining sun.

ONION

The caterpillars ate a tidy hole
In every single growing cabbage head.
Grandfather jumped about with rage.
He shouted and his face turned red.

"Kill those pesky pests," he cried.
"Stamp them, smash them, squash them flat!
I will not have my cabbage chewed!"
He yelled so loud he scared the cat.

But I don't mind those tidy holes.
I'd let the caterpillars munch,
For if they ate and ate and ate
There'd still be plenty for our lunch.

CABBAGE

Leeks for sale! Leeks for sale!
Also cabbages and kale.
Carrots, long and gold,
Lettuce to be sold,
Tomatoes sweet as honey.
Come, bring your money.
And when
You have a market then
My friends and I
Will come and buy.

LEEK

I love my mother's bed of herbs—
The pretty leaves, the spicy smell.
I help her tend the growing plants,
We keep them weeded well.

My rabbit says he likes them, too:
The scent of tarragon,
Of basil, parsley, mint, and dill,
Warmed by the summer sun.

He says it sometimes makes him feel
Under a wizard's spell,
Lulled to sleep by rosemary
And its delicious smell.

MINT

THYME

BASIL

ROSEMARY

PARSLEY

SAGE

PARSLEY

DILL

HERBS

SAGE

CHIVE

MINT

THYME

CHIVE

TARRAGON

29

"Summer will soon be over and done,"
I hear the birds say.
"Goodbye to long days of heat and of sun,
They're going away.

"Summer is passing, summer is going.
The bright petals fall.
We'll remember the flowers when it is snowing,
We'll remember them all.

"Summer will soon be done and be over,
Autumn's begun.
There are no more blooms for the bees in the clover,
Summer is over.

"But wasn't it pretty?
Wasn't it fun?"

NASTURTIUM